# All that glows has fire inside

Shayara Perera

Presentation by *BookLeaf Publishing*

Web: www.bookleafpub.com

E-mail: info@bookleafpub.com

ISBN: 978-93-95755-86-3

First edition 2022

# Flying Free

I wish I was a bird, not a bee
So my shoulders would not be burdened by all this
responsibility
The world would not stop if I ceased to be
Everything would carry on without me
Birds can fly and so can bees
But only one of them can fly truly free
The other is stuck in honey
Bound by everyone else's needs
Too much work to be done
No time to stop and breathe

# Too Young

Maybe you're too young to know
That the issue you dismiss so easily
Is the same issue that plagues the woman you love

Maybe you're too young to know
That this very plague is the same force that turns your
daughters beaming, shining bright eyes
Into dark, pointed lasers
Searching for danger she knows is just around the
corner

Maybe you're too young to know
That even being the best man still makes you an
oppressor if you
Ignore, quieten, dismiss and refuse to acknowledge
the screaming voices of women
Pleading for you to hear them out
Pleading for you to chose them over the ego that
claims you
Pleading for you to chose them over the voices of
other men telling you they are still more important
than the woman you love
Pleading for you to chose the bullied instead of the
bully
Pleading for you to chose love
Pleading for you to chose empathy
Pleading for you to chose them

Maybe I am too young to know
that even if nothing changes today
Something might change some day

But even if I am too young
I still do know
That humans are not made of black and white
I know that if we peel back the layers
Piled upon us by a society that claims to be our home
We all still have a heart
And that heart has an infinite capacity for love
Even if all it has known is hate

And even if I am young, I still have hope
That this world will one day be a better place.

# Anger

I know my sadness is always camouflaged by anger
So when my heart is heavy, I scream
People think I am screaming at them
But really I am just screaming for help

They feel the sting of my words
And think I intentionally shot the arrow
But the truth is I lost control
When the arrow shot me

Energy is heated
Atoms want out
Like a boiling kettle
This steam needs to be let out

So I run
To let my anger free
If I don't let out this carbon dioxide
It will surely consume me

But what am I running from
A problem or just me
Which is worse,
the pain in my heart or in my knees?

Had I found the wound
I would have fixed it myself
Anger won't fix it
That's why I need your help

But anger is proud
He's as tall as a hill
You're going to face some resistance
Before he lets you in

I'm pushing you away
But I need you to hold me close
Show me you still care
And that you'll always be there

Because part of me is testing
Your loyalty and my worth
The other part is kicking
Recklessly at the dirt

I know its hard
And extremely unfair
I really didn't mean
For you to end up there

As the epicentre of my rage
Anger won't stay in his cage
Run before it's to late
Because your safety I can't gauge

When the beast of anger finds me
If you can't be beside me
Then that's ok
I'll find my way

After every storm, the sun must rise
Sometimes all it takes, is some time
So when he finally leaves me
Just promise that you'll come find me

# Set her free

We've been together for a long time, you should
know by now my character
What you see is what you get, I'm not some kind of
actor
I love you, I really do,
And I've vowed to do so till the end of time too
Isn't that enough to lay this issue to rest?
So we can finally move on to help each other be our
best

Is there room to grow in this love
For the both of us?
To grow you need sunlight and water
Not doubt and a harsh border
Love is not possession, love is nuturing
How can you justify this when it's me you're hurting

It's not just you, it's me too
The two of us are bound in our cages, holding on so
tightly to each other
Both the captured and the captor
One way or another
But you should know my love
That you do not need to bind me
This bird was always going to fly home to you
All you had to do was set her free

# Let go

I need this to stop
This heartbreak
This heartache
This mind of mine that's racing
You've rattled me to my bones

I loved you, I cared for you
More than anything I was there for you
A supposed best friend of mine
Your smile I thought was sunshine

But your ego is loud
It clouds what's true
Maybe this is the end of the road
For me and you

I've apologized
But you don't see the tears I've cried
How can you see anything else
When you only have eyes for yourself

Expectations, expectations
Only of me never of you
Understand, reach out
And don't  anybody dare doubt
The superiority of your knowledge
Why would I feel the need to challenge?
Your ego got bruised?

Can't be worse than feeling used

I want to be understanding
But I tried that
And now I'm plain mad
I'm angry at you
There I said it
For the same reasons
You're mad at me too

I thought you knew me better
Didn't think you'd treat me so bitter
I don't really know what to do with you
Part of me feels like I'm through with you

I've buried my hurt
And taken responsibility
But I can do that no longer
Being your doormat is humiliating me

You seem to know it all
You drove this friendship into a wall
But you don't know what friendship means
All you know is to take and never give

You're hurt
You thought I knew you best
So when I gave you my truth
You got upset

If you can't handle feedback
Then you might as well take 3 steps back
The world will speak out loud and clear
Can you accept it, without cowering in fear?

Everyone tells me to move on
But after twelve years
How can all the memories be gone

But still, now I know
Of you, I must let go

# Men

Why is it like this? Is it their love for power?
I feel like goddamn rupunzel stuck in a tower
And it's not that I don't appreciate all that they do
But I need to be able to breathe on my own too

My dearest father, your care doesn't count for
nothing
In fact, it really counts for something
It's the care you've given me that should give you
peace of mind
That all of the lessons you have taught me aren't
forgotten behind
I know how to take care of myself, I've done it all
along
And it's important that I be able to do it even when
you're gone
You can't shield me from the world, no matter how
much you might try
You can't stop the tears when this heart wants to cry
But don't you worry, I can handle myself
I've done it all this time

And you my love, I find hard to understand
Why do you not trust the love I put in your hands
You fear less for my safety, more about another man
This gap in trust makes it feel like we are from
different lands

You do not give me credit for the loyalty I have
shown
Nor acknowledge the power I have on my own
You dismiss my autonomy and make me out to be
helpless
As though if another man came near me I'd be utterly
defenceless
But you should know I can handle it
After all, I've done it all this time

Why is that they still treat me like I am so fragile
Handle with utmost care reads the sign
But I've handled it on my own all this time
Please give me the space to breathe and shine
I can handle it myself
I've done it all this time

# Free

I want to break free
Freedom speaks out to me
You've got to break these shackles
Under this pressure you will buckle
Take time to breathe
It's ok to just be
You do not always have to do
Or make sure that you prove
That you are worthy to walk on this land
Perhaps it's time we all take a stand
Life is for living
But this nine to five is just killing
For what?
Taking a risk we resist
Just to exist
Until time runs out
And only the sun is left to pout

# Feeling like a ghost

All I can see are the flaws in your soul
You are still mine but you don't feel like my own
I want to remember the love I once felt
The feeling that you were my one and only best friend
To feel safe in your arms
Not shroud my cold heart
To feel the warmth of your hand in mine
Lighting my body, knowing we were ours
To sleep soundly at night, just because you were next to me
To feel like eating to my heart's content because I was just so happy
To feel that I was enough, because you loved me so damn much
To feel like I could conquer the world because you were there to lift me up
What happened, where did you go?
I know your love is knocking at my door
But I just can't open it
My heart is hurt and my body heavy
I feel like a ghost, the real me buried

# Dear Future Teller

I know you are not supposed to know the future
But I just need to know
That there is something more
Than the drudgery of this nine to five
How can I die
Satisfied with the life I've lived
If I have no time to give
Back to those who love me
And even those who don't
Just because they don't
Doesn't mean I won't
So please, tell me
We will have time to stop and be
To stop and breathe
And be truely present
Appreciate each other's presence
Not take a moment for granted
It is agony to be parted
From the ones you love
And the things you love
Life cannot be such a chore
I will not accept it anymore
Surely you can't expect me to believe
That this was all life was meant to be

# Childhood Friends

Anger and sadness here you are again
Since my childhood we've been well acquainted
friends
So what brings you back?
Who here got attacked?
You worry my mother you know?
But you don't worry me anymore
You've come and you've gone
And though when you leave it's hard to move on
I've learnt to let go
Had glimmers of hope
I know what you're trying to do but I don't need your
protection
I have long since  made my peace with imperfections
But I promise I won't judge you
Because I have truly known you
You were my comfort zone
There's things that only the three of us know
But I just wish you could see
The destruction you cause around me
You hurt the people I love
So when push comes to shove
I will choose them
And for them
I will try to be a better me

# Loud Speak

There is no room for tolerating
Applaud awarded only for aggravating
You are weak if you do not speak your mind
But anger is what makes you blind
I am dynamite
Do not light your flames near me
Fireworks is not what you will see
But the sting of a burn you will feel
And by then it may be too late
Kindness too can have strength
Don't blame me if I am silent
It's taken years to cut this anger down to a tenth

# Breaking Point

I scream at you to care
But you scream back that you don't care
Most times it's like you're not there
The love we shared feels scarce
How old are we? Five?
Cause you're acting like a child
Boys need to grow into men
Your wives cannot always fend
And tend
Money is not everything
Caring has to count for something
The scale is not equal
Is this the prequel
To a life of misery
The way you hurt me can't you see
The male ego is blind
My heart always tried to be kind
But we all reach a point
When the effort is not joint
I cannot do any more
Soul is just too sore
Don't blame me when the towel is in
I gave you my everything
Some words you can't take back
Foundation is starting to crack
But you refuse to see
You just want to 'be'
Stagnant

Something I'd hate to be
So you continue being lazy
I'll keep my eyes hazy
One day this string might snap
And we won't make it back

# Ignore

It's pathetic I'd say
That I can't even make it a day
Without talking to you
When it comes so easily to you
You get occupied with work
With life
But I only ignore you out of spite
Because here I am trying my best to be alone
Yet you still occupy my mind like it's your own
How do you do it?
What is your trick
Please help this fickle mind of mine
Pretend like you don't exist
But what's the point in that?
You won't notice even if I succeed
For you to notice, you'd have to actually see

# Just Remember

Some of us have found the one
The rest of us are on the run
From ourselves
From someone
Because we don't know what to do
There's just too much to lose
If we stop and change paths
We risk being judged
When all we need is a hug
All we get is a shrug
And the words of trivialisation
Serve as a reminder
That we must be kinder
To ourselves
Because no one else will fight this battle
This is our sphere to rattle
Don't heed their advice
Your problems won't be solved by being nice
Just believe
And use your powers to perceive the truth
Your time will come
Just remember to breathe it through

# Nothing to Overthink

I don't want to overthink love
But every time I'm happy, I wait for the
Shoe to drop
I brace for impact
But it never quite comes
Somehow we always manage to stay as one
When did I become such a pessimist
Why do I always fear like this
Head spinning, Heart racing
Won't sit down
Can't stop pacing
Taking a leap
Makes me feel weak
Love can be dangerous
Maybe that's why it's for the courageous
But whatever is said and done
We all still need someone
I thank my lucky stars
I never have to look too far
Because time after time
I continue to find
For every reason I've given you to walk away
You always find one to stay

# glad you stay

Sometimes I wonder
Why you choose to stay
After all the pain that won't fade away
Every scar etched on your heart
The words withheld
The silent spells
The bouts of rage
Can't move past this page
In a loop
Losing hope
Want you close but feel apart
Love is just a painful art
We feel the same
Yet you wait for my sunnier days
And for that
In my heart you'll always hold a place

# Mine for a Moment

All I'm asking for is a moment
Where your mind is mine
We forget about time
And responsibilities and life
And just sit
The world could be falling apart
But we find our sync
Somewhere a fire could start
But we let our hearts beat
The light may not shine through the dark
But we let our lungs breathe
We may have no control
But for a moment we just stop and be
For a moment
All I want is you and me

# Dance with me

Will you dance with me?
In the middle of a busy street
Or alone under a starry fleet
Outdoors, when the weather is warm
Just the two of us?

Will you dance with me?
In the middle of the night
Adorned by the bed light
Everyone asleep, not a single soul in sight
Just the two of us?

Will you dance with me?
In the middle of cooking
Where no one is looking
We can get lost in our own little world
Just the two of us

Will you dance with me today?
Because these legs might not work one day
So will you hold me close and sway?
Can you love me in that way?

# Alone is okay

I want you to know
That even if you are alone
You will be okay
You don't need anyone to stay
But yourself
Let nature engulf you
Embrace the adventure that beckons you
There is so much of this world unexplored
Experiences knocking at your door
The world is excited to see you
So many people would love to meet you
And know your heart
The world is full of art for you to make meaning of
Open your arms and welcome love
Friendships with strangers make for beautiful stories
And you will forever cherish these memories
Open your eyes
Inside you there is still a child
Who is just looking for happiness
Please grant them this
Surpass your limits, let go of your fear
This is what life is about
And you only have one
So make it count

# Home is a person

Sometimes I feel your eyes on me
While my eyes are watching the screen
I wonder what you are thinking
But I like it that you are looking
The language of hearts
Is loudest in silence
It's not every day that you come by this
Type of connection
It may not be perfection
But it is what's right
Just hold on to me tight
In this ride
Called life
We will fall and we will stand
Just don't let go of my hand
We will make it through
Even if we are one of the few
Because you are my home
I know it in my bones

# Meet me there

Will you meet me there
Where our souls can be bare
No walls, no doors to knock down
We meet each other with understanding not a frown

Will you meet me there
Where we leave all judgements behind
Only know how to be kind
Let our ears truly listen
As our eyes glisten when we finally break through
our hurdles

Will you meet me there
Where we talk without holding back
Realise that there's nothing to attack
Admit we are both to blame
But our team is still the same

Will you meet me there
Where the winter air
Is cold but the summer sun shines through
We understand the rule of twos:
Everything must be in balance

Will you meet me there
Where we are both finally aware
This world is a catastrophe
But let's change the ending shall we?

www.ingramcontent.com/pod-product-compliance
Lightning Source LLC
LaVergne TN
LVHW021346200726
843509LV00014B/2700